Preparedness for EMP Attack and Solar Storms

A Survival Guide to EMP Weapons, Electromagnetic Pulse, Solar Storms, Solar Flares and Carrington Events

Steve Rayder

I0417532

Steve Rayder

www.southshorepublications.com

© 2015 by SouthShore Publications & Distribution.

ISBN- 978-1512332933

ISBN-10: 1512332933

Steve Rayder

CONTENTS

1. INTRODUCTION   PG. 7

2. TYPES OF EMP AND THE EFFECTS   PG. 11

3. EMP MYTHS   PG. 15

4. IMMEDIATE SURVIVAL   PG. 18

5. FINDING AND TREATING WATER   PG. 22

6. OTHER PEOPLE   PG. 27

7. POTASSIUM IODIDE AND RADIATION   PG. 31

8. EMP PROTECTION AND FARADAY CAGES   PG. 34

9. ELECTRICAL ITEMS YOU SHOULD PROTECT   PG. 38

10. LONG TERM SURVIVAL   PG. 42

11. GENERATING YOUR OWN ELECTRICITY   PG. 46

12. FINAL THOUGHTS   PG. 49

Steve Rayder

1. INTRODUCTION

EMPs or electromagnetic pulses are an electromagnetic disturbances that can damage and disrupt electrical equipment.

Our society's vulnerability to EMP's and Solar Storms began a long time ago, in the 1880's, with Nikola Tesla. His discoveries caused us to have an alternating current power grid in order to cut down on the amount of power stations needed to supply electricity to the population. This also allows us to transmit electricity over huge distances using power lines and transformers. This is a great system and it was chosen for good reason, but it is vulnerable.

It's quite amazing if you think about it. This huge web of cables reaching all over the country delivering electricity to everyone who needs it whenever they need it at the flip of a switch. The system was built to function well and it does. The only problem is, the people making this system work so well, didn't really give a whole lot of thought to security.

There is actually pretty much no protection for the grid in reality. No one in power seems to pay much attention to this fact either. If a war were to break out at any point, in theory it would actually be pretty easy for another country to knock out the transformers and render our entire electrical grid useless. This would cause not only the loss of most forms of communication but it would also cause widespread panic throughout the population.

So if the government spends so much on national security and the armed forces, why would they leave such a gaping hole in our defenses for any would be enemies to exploit? Well, there is no one who is actually responsible for the security of the grid. The government don't own it. The companies who run the grid don't want any added expenses. Yet again it's all about money and big business, just like everything else these days it seems. These companies don't want to foot the bill for implementing additional security measures.

You may be thinking, why don't the government make them do it? Well there is currently no regulatory body set up to deal with this issue. Of course the companies have replacement transformers. But not enough to replace all of them, not even close. They can't just make new ones quickly either as they're very complex pieces of engineering and they aren't currently manufactured in house anyway. So if anything were to happen to the transformers, there would be no quick fix or easy way out.

The most likely weapon that could be used to take down the grid is an electromagnetic pulse weapon. Sounds sci-fi but they are real weapons, they have been made and tested. They work and could easily be used in a modern day warfare situation. There was a test of an EMP weapon at high altitude over the Pacific Ocean in 1962. This test caused damage in Hawaii which was many miles away.

EMP isn't even a new invention, the sun actually gives off an extremely large electromagnetic pulses every century or two on average in what is sometimes called a Carrington Event, solar flare or solar storm. These solar storms are so large in fact that they can interfere with the electromagnetic field of the earth in quite a dramatic fashion. Even the much smaller solar storms cause issues, so the next large one or even a small one hitting a highly populated area could cause us some real problems.

It's not just the grid that would be damaged by an EMP however. There are three types of EMP. So maybe just the grid will go down, or maybe all electrical equipment within the radius would be damaged, down to the electrical components of vehicles meaning even your car wouldn't start. Maybe even both.

So with this in mind, and the electrical grid as vulnerable as it is, the only option we have if we want to be ready for this, is to prepare ourselves as best we can.

Steve Rayder

2. TYPES OF EMP AND THE EFFECTS

As I mentioned, there are three types of EMP. The first is lighting, which I'm sure doesn't need much explaining. This type of electromagnetic pulse is capable of causing huge amounts of physical damage, but as we are fairly familiar with it, we generally know how to protect ourselves from it.

The second is the low frequency, long wavelength pulse. This type of pulse is what solar storms from the sun consist of. They are essentially highly energized particles. That contain every ray of light including gamma rays and x-rays. These rays are dangerous but they will be absorbed by the earth's atmosphere acting as a shield to protect us from their harmful effects. This is the type of pulse that would cause major problems to the electrical grid. So I would say this is the most likely scenario as you have the risk of a man made EMP weapon producing this pulse, but also the risk of solar storms.

Solar storm is starting to sound more and more far-fetched the more I say it. Let me give you a quick example to prove that these things do happen. In 1858 there was a larger than usual Solar Storm. The electromagnetic pulse it created hit the earth and some of the energy was picked up and passed along by the Telegraph lines as this was pretty much the only advanced technology they had. This actually caused the Telegraph lines to burn. Luckily back then, the damage would have been a lot easier to repair. But if it happened now, it wouldn't be so easy. Not by a long shot.

It's also worth mentioning that it's likely that an EMP weapon would be in missile form. More specifically a nuclear bomb detonated over the target area, as nuclear explosions will emit a strong EMP. Of course in most developed countries, since the 1960's, we have had advanced anti-missile systems. So this offers some form of protection to the grid, but this doesn't stop solar storms.

So let's say this type of EMP occurred and caused the grid to go down, what exactly would happen? As discussed the electrical grid would go down. This means the lights would go out, possibly also including emergency lighting. Obviously our computers, televisions, etc. wouldn't have any power meaning a loss of communication. But also the water plants and sewage systems are powered by electricity so our basic needs for water and sanitation would also become a problem.

There would be mass looting and scavenging for supplies in the days and weeks after an EMP. Water would very quickly become a major concern for everyone. It would basically be chaos. We would most likely see mass migrations of people leaving overcrowded cities and crime levels would rise dramatically.

The third is a long frequency, short wavelength pulse and is more likely to be caused by an EMP weapon that can also give off the long wavelength EMP. This type of pulse is what causes damage to all kinds of electrical equipment. With this type of EMP attack. Everything from our laptops and phones to our cars could potentially all be rendered useless.

This would cause the same type of mass panic and looting as the last type of EMP. So both of the last two types of EMP would be disastrous for the majority of the population. I say the majority because the government have measures to keep themselves safe in almost all circumstances. Some of the incredibly rich 1% also have bunkers that will withstand pretty much anything so they will be fine too provided they can get to them. So if we want to have the best chance of survival as possible, we need to have a plan too.

Steve Rayder

3. EMP MYTHS

So now we know about the different types of EMP and how they could be caused, I wanted to go over some myths and common misconceptions about EMP that are thrown about a lot by Preppers on forums etc.

There are rumors floating about that you need a specialist EMP bomb or a very powerful bomb in order to create enough EMP to effect a wide area and knock out electrical equipment. Tests have actually shown that any kind of nuclear bomb will create high levels of EMP, enough to wipe out most of the electronic equipment in the whole of the United States with just one bomb detonated at high altitude.

Some people will tell you that as long as your electrical equipment isn't attached to a long piece of metal such as an antenna or cable, it will be safe. Now there is some truth in this as long pieces of metal will be affected much more than shorter pieces, but smaller items can still be damaged.

The next myth is that all cars will suddenly stop working. This is partially true as some cars would just stop dead, but not all of them. There are two main reasons that some cars will still work after an EMP. Reason one is that the electronics in cars are pretty well shielded for health and safety reasons. Also cars are made from metal which will provide a Faraday Effect to help protect the internal electronics so they will have some protection from the pulse. So some cars will stop working, some will need repairs, some will be damaged but still run and some will be fine. Unfortunately there hasn't been much testing on this so it's hard to say how many cars will be effected exactly.

I have heard people saying that if you have an old radio with a vacuum tube, it won't be affected by an EMP. This would be great if it were true but in actual fact there is no truth behind this one at all. There has been testing on this subject and vacuum tube equipment was damaged by EMP.

Another myth is that microwaves can save your electrics from being destroyed by and EMP if you put them inside. People prove this by placing their phone inside and them trying to call it. When it doesn't work they say that it proves that it is protected. This isn't true unfortunately, if they had used an AM radio with a strong signal and put that in there instead, they would have heard it still playing because it's not protected enough from this wavelength.

Another common myth seems to be that it wouldn't take long to repair the grid if it was fried by an EMP. The fact is, the transformers would take a very long time to replace, estimates range up to 10 years to replace them all although I would say a likely time frame to repair the whole grid would probably be about 5 years and it would cost billions. These transformers weigh about 70 tons and they take about 6 months to replace even now. So to replace hundreds at once, that's going to take years.

4. IMMEDIATE SURVIVAL

If an EMP were to go off and cause our electrics to go into overload. There would be some very immediate dangers to consider. This depends dramatically on where you are and what you are doing at the time the EMP hits.

If you are inside a large building such as an office block or high up in a block of flats then you will need to get out as soon as possible. Why is it such a pressing concern to get out? Because the overloaded electrics in the building could quite easily start a fire with you inside. With all the lights and possibly the emergency lighting gone, and with everyone rushing for the exits in the dark stair wells, this could be a much harder task than it sounds.

So, tip number one for EMP survival is to carry a flashlight on you at all times and hope it doesn't get fried by the electromagnetic pulse. The smaller the flashlight, the better the chance it will survive the electromagnetic pulse. There's not really any excuse not to have one on you at all times, especially with the range of tiny keychain flashlights that are available on the market today. As part of my EDC (Everyday Carry) I keep a small LED flashlight on my keychain and it's incredibly useful anyway just in everyday life. If you would like a recommendation then the Streamlight Nano is a very popular choice.

If you're in a car and you're driving at the time, there is a possibility that a lot of the cars on the road may suddenly stop working. This could lead to pile ups and crashes, which would make the roads very dangerous. Also if you're one of the only people with a working car, you're going to become a target for anyone desperate enough to try and take it from you. So if you are on the road and your car is still working, stay on the side roads and try to get home as quickly as possible in order to draw as little attention to yourself as possible. A good idea would probably also be to park up in a secluded spot near to your home and walk the rest of the way rather than boldly pulling up in your working car in front of your entire street.

Also if you're tempted to stop off and get some gas for your car, there will be no point. The pumps won't be working because they run on electricity. Just like every other shop they will close the shutters when the power goes down and deny access to anyone.

So avoiding the immediate dangers that would threaten your life in the minutes following the EMP, the next thing to do is to determine what exactly has happened and make sure this isn't just a power cut. The main clue you will have is the lack of radio stations so try your radio. If you don't have one or your is broken ask anyone nearby to check theirs. I will talk about keeping a protected radio later in the book.

It will be worth checking your phone, it may well be dead but there is a chance it could still be working. You would expect the network to be down but they do actually have battery backups so you may still be able to contact family members and friends for a time in order to get everyone together safely. Time will be of the essence. This also means that just because some phones are still working, it doesn't necessarily mean there hasn't been an EMP.

You do have one distinct advantage over most other people. Everyone else is going to be standing around scratching their heads wondering what's going on thinking there has been some kind of weird power cut. Seeing as you know what's happening and you have educated yourself on the topic, you will know what to do.

The first thing I would suggest to do if you are at home and something like this occurs and you think it could be an EMP, is to check that there are no fires in your home caused by malfunctioning electronics. For this reason it is vital to have at least one fire extinguisher in your home. It's best to have more than one stored in different locations. This is because a fire could break out in the room with the fire extinguisher in or a fire could block your path stopping you from getting to it. With no emergency services available or maybe not even contactable, seeing as the phones may be down and they will be dealing with everything else that's going on, you will need to be able to deal with fires in your home by yourself. So get a couple of fire extinguishers and keep them in separate areas of your home.

Your next immediate concern should be water. With the grid down the water won't be pumping for long or it may have already stopped. So fill up any containers you can along with your bath and your sink. If you can, fill up some bin liners or condoms or anything else that holds water. You want to save as much water as you can as fast as you can, this is a major factor that will enable to you to survive for as long as possible in the safety of your home while everyone else is forced out of town in order to find water.

In our day to day lives it is estimated that we use around 50 gallons of water a day each for general washing and eating etc. In a survival situation we need about 2 gallons each but you could get away with one gallon if you were very careful with it.

5. FINDING AND TREATING WATER

If you're lucky enough to live in a rural area, you will most likely find it a lot easier than most to collect water, especially if you live close to a river or lake. People in urban areas are going to find it much harder.

The idea really is to just collect as much as you can and store it away in your home. The people that don't have the foresight to do this, who maybe thought this was just a power cut, will now have to start moving out of cities and towns in search of fresh water sources in less populated areas. This is where the people in rural locations start to encounter problems.

Many experts predict that in a disaster scenario such as this, there would be mass migrations of people. In the case of an EMP this will likely occur mainly on foot if a lot of cars are no longer functional. So the people who think they are safe in their unpopulated area with their river nearby will soon encounter a horde of city goers descending upon their water source. Not only drinking it but also washing in it. Chances are there are also going to be some idiots who think it's a good idea to use a river or a lake as a bathroom causing some serious contamination issues, especially with water that isn't flowing.

Luckily for us, it may not rain money or a lot else for that matter but it does rain water. Seeing as water is essential to our survival it's quite handy that it just falls out of the sky. If you have tarps you can set up rain water collectors that are very effective. You can also put containers under your downpipes to collect water.

This is my next big tip on being prepared, if you have a garden, set up a series of water butts to collect rain water in advance. This could literally one day save your life. If you want to be extra well prepared you could house them in some sort of shelter or shed with a lock. This will stop people who are desperately searching for water from poking their head over your garden fence, seeing your water butts and taking your water.

The amount of water butts you need depends on the amount or rain fall you get in your part of the world. It will also depend on the season and the amount of people in your home that you will need water for. The water you collect this way might not be the cleanest water in the world but it can be filtered and boiled to make it safe for human consumption.

To filter water you ideally want to have a decent water filter. I'm not talking about a Britta water filter or something like that. You need something much stronger. The first choice of many preppers is a Berkey Filtration System. They are basically a big metal cylinder. You put the dirty water in the top and it comes out the bottom clean. The great thing about these filters is that they are powered by nothing more than gravity, so even with the power down, they will serve you well.

You can even put swimming pool or river water into a Berkey and it will come out ready to drink. They really are the best filters available on the market in my opinion and they are a must have item. If you're going to buy anything for your house to get prepared, make it one of these.

If you need to prepare water for drinking in a more primitive way then you have a couple of options. Firstly, you will need to get any sediment and as much of the chemicals and contaminants out of the water as possible. To do this you will need to rig up some kind of filtration system. To do this you will first need some sort of housing for the filter, an upturned bottle with the base removed is commonly used for this. Then you will need to plug the nozzle with some cloth to keep the filter media in place. Next you should add some charcoal from a fire. Charcoal is full of tiny holes that will help remove any of the microscopic contaminants. Next you should add a layer of sand as this will remove any smaller particles in the water. Finally you can add something like grass to remove the larger pieces of dirt in the water if you want to.

You can also filter water through a strip of cloth using gravity. To do this you will need two containers. Put the first container filled with the dirty water on a higher level with the empty container below it. Next put a strip of material into the first container and hanging down into the empty container. The water will soak up into the fabric and be drawn down, eventually dripping into the second container. This will take some time, but it will separate the water from most of the dirt and sediment.

Next you will need to boil your water in order to kill off any pathogens that may be contained in it. This is essential for any kind of water that may be contaminated with feces such as water from rivers, lakes and ponds. You should boil the water for at least 3 minutes or 5 if you are at high altitudes, as water boils faster and at lower temperatures the higher you get.

Of course, with the power out, those of you with electric stoves won't be able to boil water inside and gas probably won't be working either. So you will have to get back to basics and make a fire to boil your water over. Fires will draw attention to you and in urban areas, you're not going to have a lot to burn. What you do have will go quickly seeing as you will now be relying on fires for cooking, warmth and water purification.

The other option is to use bleach or iodine to purify your water. Bleach is useful for making water safe to drink without the use of fire. This may sound dangerous as obviously drinking bleach generally isn't a great idea, but it's actually not dangerous when it is highly diluted and not done for an extremely extended time period. It will however destroy anything harmful in the water.

Add 4 drops of bleach per liter of warm water and leave it to sit for half an hour. If you can't warm your water in any way then just double the dose but it will taste quite bleachy.

Iodine can also be used in the same way and it's safer for human consumption than bleach. Side note, it is recommended that you don't use Iodine for water purification for longer 6 months straight. If you don't like the taste of Iodine you can use vitamin C tablets as they will neutralize the Iodine and make your water taste a lot better.

So overall, my preparedness advice regarding water in an EMP scenario would be:

- Store some water for immediate usage.

- Fill up any containers you have including your bath and sinks while the water is still on.

- Set up a system of water butts to collect rain water if possible.

- Get a Berkey Water Filter for effective filtration without electricity, chemicals or fire.

6. OTHER PEOPLE

At first, when people are still figuring out what is going on and before the panic starts, people will be friendly. It's estimated this friendliness will last about 4 hours. After 4 hours however, this is the point where panic sets in and people will begin to loot and take whatever they can get their hands on if they think it may improve their chances of survival.

If you think that the police force will be able to maintain order for longer than 4 hours then I am sorry to say, it's fairly certain that they won't. If a police officer is driving along and suddenly his car, radio and phone die, he is going to be just as confused as everyone else. They will also be far more concerned with getting home to check their families are safe rather than dealing with all of the people who are approaching him asking him what's going on. Especially when he has nothing to tell them.

During hurricane Katrina, half of the police force in the area abandoned their duties and went to take care of their families. In that situation they knew what was happening. Imagine how many would give up and go back home if something incredibly strange and confusing like this happened. Combine this with the fact that they probably have no way of communicating with them to make sure they are okay, I would say close to all police and other emergency service personnel would walk straight out of their jobs and head home.

So you would be wise to use the first four hours to get ahead of the game. Get your family together first, then get as many supplies as you can and get back home before the chaos ensues.

After the four hours and for the foreseeable future, the streets will not be safe. Make no mistake, there are people who will have guns and other weapons. They will take whatever they can from other people. If you're in your home this at least offers you some level of security and comfort.

The first few days before the reality of the situation sinks in for most people will be dangerous but not as bad as it will be in the coming weeks.

Essentially the longer the situation lasts for, the more desperate people will be come. The more desperate people are, the more dangerous they will become. So it makes sense to pull together with people you know and neighbors to form a community that can help to defend each other if you need to. I know it's a cliché but there is safety in numbers so form a group of people who you can trust. Family members are best for this as they are far less likely to stab you in the back, but a large group of neighbors coming together and forming a defensive group against any roaming armed gangs will be an effective deterrent.

I have heard people say that an EMP attack would essentially send us back in time to the 1800's. People would have to form small communities. They would have to learn to govern and protect themselves. Other than defense and some form of rules and law among the community, there would also be the huge benefit of shared information. For example, there may be a doctor or a surgeon in this group of people who could provide expert medical advice to the rest of the group. You will be someone who will bring value due to the fact that you are obviously the kind of person who would have researched, and therefore know what to do in situations like this.

I personally think that comparing the post EMP world to the 1800s is inaccurate. It would be far worse than the 1800s. I say this because back then, people knew how to feed themselves and find water. These days most people can't look after their own basic survival needs. Due to our reliance on modern society, most of the vital skills we would need to survive something like this have been lost to most of us.

Countless people will die in the months after an EMP. People who require specialist medications and medical care would be the first to go. Dehydration and drinking dirty water would also be a big killer. Then starvation would begin to kill a lot of people too. If you think about the amount of people there are these days, there won't be anywhere near enough food to forage, and most wild animals will be hunted to near extinction in under a year. This means there will be hardly any animals to hunt before long. Even domestic animals like dogs, cats and horses will be eaten.

The people who will survive will be the ones who are best prepared and the ones who form strong communities with good plans that will enable food and water to be grown, stored and collected efficiently.

7. POTASSIUM IODIDE AND RADIATION

If the EMP came from a nuclear weapon detonated at high altitude over the country, there would be some nuclear fallout as a result. You will need something to protect yourself and your family from the effects of the nuclear radiation.

Earlier in the book, in the water chapter I mentioned that you could use Iodine to make water safe to drink. Well Iodine actually has another useful application in a nuclear disaster. Iodine is absorbed by your thyroid and will protect it against radiation.

The most effective way to protect yourself from radiation however is to keep some Potassium Iodide tablets on standby in case you need them. The CDC actually recommends keeping Potassium Iodide in your emergency supplies. When the power station at Chernobyl went into melt down they saved a lot of lives by giving out Potassium Iodide tablets to those who were in the fallout zone.

It basically works by filling your thyroid so that the radiation has nowhere to go. The younger you are, the more at risk you are of developing problems from radiation. Young children are at extremely high risk. So if you have children, you should definitely get some.

As a side note, it's worth remembering that there are nuclear power stations all over the world and wind can carry radiation great distances. When nuclear power plants have some kind of disaster you can't get hold of Iodine or Potassium Iodide for any amount of money. It will be completely sold out everywhere, so it's worth getting some anyway.

I would suggest taking a look at the Iosat brand, they come very highly recommended. They come in blister packs of 14 tablets. This is intended for 1 person, taking one tablet per day for 14 days, so you will need to pick up a pack for each of your family members. You could also get some extra packs as these will be so valuable if any kind of nuclear disaster of EMP attack were to occur. This will enable you to barter with them in exchange for food and other supplies.

They do have an expiry date on them, but to be honest, this is just a way for drug companies to make more money by telling people they need to replace perfectly good medication. Also, even if they are years past their expiry date, in a disaster scenario, you're still going to be glad you have them.

Another thing that can help in a nuclear fallout is staying inside and sealing all doors and windows. You should also keep surgical masks to help filter the air you're breathing. Rosemary has been found to offer good protection from radiation poisoning. Rosemary extract could be used as a medication.

Mainly I would suggest the tablets as they are fairly inexpensive and are proven to work very effectively.

8. EMP PROTECTION AND FARADAY CAGES

A Faraday Cage is a container that protects its contents from electrical fields, charges and EMP. You can buy commercially made Faraday Cages but they are very expensive. Luckily it's not too hard to make your own.

Essentially a Faraday Cage is just a metal container preferably made from Copper or Aluminum. There is a lot of talk among preppers about wrapping their electrical gear in plastic and then a layer of aluminum foil to protect it from EMP. The fact is that most of these preppers will be sadly disappointed when they unwarp their electrical equipment to find they don't work.

If were talking about a huge solar storm or an EMP attack that is large enough to knock out most electronics or the electrical grid, then a plastic bag and a layer of foil isn't going to be enough to stop the EMP from frying the circuits in your electrical equipment.

Now, don't get me wrong, it will help and it may save your items if you're far enough away from the source of the blast. The idea behind this is that the foil will absorb the pulse and dissipate it while the non-conductive plastic stops the pulse from reaching the electrical device inside it. The principle is good, but a layer of foil and a plastic bag probably won't be enough protection.

You will need a good 5 layers of properly wrapped aluminum foil around a non-conductive layer such as paper or plastic in order to create a good enough Faraday Effect to effectively protect your equipment. It's also very important that you properly seal the edges of the foil and ensure there are no rips in the foil. If you leave any gaps there is a much higher chance that the pulse will find its way through.

A very important note about this method is not to place anything between the 5 foil layers. These layers of foil must be touching each other.

This should be enough to protect most electronics but personally I would also recommend nesting your Faraday cages to ensure they are completely safe. What I mean by nesting is essentially putting your wrapped items inside another Faraday Cage. The easiest way to do this for smaller items like radios is to simply place them inside a shoe box and wrap that in a further 5 layers of foil.

You could also contain all of the the individually wrapped items inside a galvanized steel trash can. You will need to insulate the inside so that the foil wrapped items don't touch the inside metal surface of the trash can, cardboard is good for this. The trash can will act as the first Faraday cage and whatever pulse gets through will be significantly weaker and should definitely be effectively dissipated by the aluminum foil wrapping the individual items.

One thing I will say about the trash can method, and a mistake I can see a lot of people making, is that you don't want the insulating material to stop the lid connecting with the body of the trash can properly. You need a good tight fit for the lid with the metal touching all the way around properly.

Another mistake that people could potentially make is to leave cables or antennas protruding from the Faraday Cage. If any part of the device, or anything that is connected to it, is protruding from the foil then it will transfer the energy it gathers into the device.

Some people also suggest using Mylar bags to protect your electrical items. This does dampen signals slightly but it won't act as an effective Faraday Cage and it definitely isn't as effective, or in fact as cost effective, as Aluminum foil.

I think what a lot of people will do if an EMP weapon did hit is to get their protected gear out and see if it works. I wouldn't do this personally, there may be multiple EMP pulses so I would wait at least 24 hours before unpacking my protected items. They probably know a lot of people would have protected some equipment, or they may be setting off two just to be sure that it worked properly.

Of course the other solution to this problem is to pack two of everything, that way you won't have to wait and see if there is another pulse, you can just get your gear out straight away and have a backup on standby for a second pulse. This gives you the advantage of being able to tune into any emergency broadcasts or communicate via radio straight away.

9. ELECTRIAL ITEMS YOU SHOULD PROTECT

A radio will give you a huge advantage and is probably the most important bit of kit that you will want to store in a Faraday Cage.

Radios are useful for gathering information by tuning into emergency radio broadcasts that will shed some light on the situation at hand. They are also great for long range communication when all other forms of communication are gone.

There are a lot of different types of radio that you may want to consider storing such as CB, GMRS, FRS, HAM, Shortwave, etc.

Shortwave radio is great for long range communication as the radio waves are reflected back to earth by the ionosphere meaning the waves can reach around the curvature of the earth without being blocked. This will enable to communicate with other people very far away and see what is going on in other countries. This could be very valuable information, especially if you are on the road or are planning on moving and are trying to work out where the best place to go would be.

The likelihood is that, other than maybe an emergency government broadcast playing on a loop, there won't be much on the airwaves that is close to you. So the long distance capabilities of Shortwave will be very useful.

The next item you should consider protecting is one or more flashlights. Not only do they contain electrical components but

LEDs are very likely to be damaged if exposed to an EMP. The older style flashlights with the old style lightbulbs should be fairly immune to an EMP but the advantages of an LED flashlight certainly warrant keeping one stored and protected from EMP.

A lot can be said for the humble flashlight, you don't want to be without a portable light source in a survival situation that's for sure. So I would say at least one LED flashlight is a must.

Any spare electrical parts for cars, such as fuses and spark plugs, should all be wrapped in foil and nested in your main container. Having these spare parts could mean that you are one of the only people with a working vehicle. This will give you a huge advantage over everyone else, meaning you can get to supplies and locations that may contain valuable resources before most other people. It also enables you to move large amounts of supplies and gear quickly and easily when most other people will only be able to take what they can carry with them.

If you want to keep any kind of specialist equipment such as night vision goggles, these will also need to be wrapped and nested for optimum protection. I would actually highly recommend a pair of night vision goggles. If you need to defend your home at night from anyone who may be trying to steal your supplies, this will give you a very good tactical advantage. Remember, almost all forms of lighting will be destroyed. So anyone trying to break into houses in the night we probably be doing so under nothing but moonlight making it pretty difficult. If you have a pair of night vision goggles, you hugely increase your chances of being able to get the jump on them and successfully defend your home.

They will also give you the advantage of being able to travel or go looking for supplies under cover of darkness when everyone else is practically blind to everything going on outside. So they would be a really great item to have.

A common question that I hear people asking a lot is if they need to protect their batteries and are they damaged in an EMP? Well, they are pretty small so they should be fine. Tests have been done and in past disasters batteries have come out undamaged so you can be pretty sure they will be okay. Even larger batteries such as car batteries may be fine. But it never hurts to make sure and wrap some batteries up and store them with the rest of your gear.

The best type of batteries to store are Energizer Ultimate Lithium as they can last in storage for up to 20 years. The Energizer AA's last 20 years, the AAA's also last 20 years and the 9 volt lasts for 10 in storage. Regular alkaline batteries should last 5-7 years so that's still not bad and you could just start out by getting some of them, but I think it's worth going for the 20 year cover personally, especially as that's going to be a lower end estimate so they are probably more likely to last for something like 30 years.

Another tip for you that is very important is to make sure you take the batteries out of the equipment you are storing before you wrap it up. If you leave the batteries in the gear you run the risk of the batteries leaking inside your expensive equipment and rendering it useless with or without the EMP.

Another side note that is worth mentioning is that if you're planning on using energy-saving CFL bulbs or equipment that uses them to cut down on wasted electricity, which isn't a bad idea by the way, keep in mind that they do have some circuitry in them so they are susceptible to EMP too.

10. LONG TERM SURVIVAL

As I mentioned, an EMP attack could cause you to be in a survival situation for the foreseeable future. If no aid comes from other countries, you will probably have to survive, medicate and feed yourself for at least a couple of years.

I would suggest keeping any survival information that you may need during an EMP either in the form of printed books or by printing it out and keeping it in a folder.

The things you may want to keep hard copies of are books on homesteading and growing your own food year round and information on preserving food for the colder months. This information could well be lifesaving.

One thing that a lot of people seem to forget about when they're buying these books about growing your own food is the fact that they need the tools and the seeds. They just tend to get a book on it and think they will just read it when the time comes. So have a read and see exactly what you're going to need to effectively be able to grow your own food in advance and get those supplies ready.

Of course the best thing you can do to get prepared for not being able to just pop down the shop anymore is to stockpile rice and beans. I will admit, plain rice and beans is not the tastiest thing in the world but it does sustain life for extended periods of time. You should also keep sugar, salt and honey. I go into this topic in more detail in my book on Bugging In and Home Defense if you would like to find out more about food storage.

Medical information will also give you a much better chance of survival. As far as medication goes there are a few legal options that you can keep with your emergency supplies that will enable you to treat a range of injuries and illnesses.

Essential oils are a fantastic natural remedy that can treat anything from viruses like colds and flus, fungal infections, bacterial infections and much more. If you keep a range of essential oils along with printed information on what each of them does, you will have a way of treating a lot of common health issues.

You can also, perfectly legally, buy fish antibiotics that are coincidentally exactly the same as the pills that you would get over the counter with a prescription.

If you have a bug out location then you should keep a physical map with alternate routes to that location, as you don't know what the condition of the roads will be like after an EMP. Many roads may be blocked by cars that have broken down or if there is rioting and looting they may be covered in debris. Another possibility is that people may set up road blocks so that they can try to trap and take the car and supplies of anyone trying to drive down that particular road.

Your car may also not be working so you should plan out a good discrete route that you can take on foot, or even better, via bicycle. I think bicycles are a fantastic long term transportation method and something that every prepper should have.

Not only will they allow you pass through the gaps in the cars and take narrow footpaths but they are much more reliable than cars and don't require fuel. They will also enable you to outrun anyone who may try to attack you if they are on foot, so it's much safer and faster than walking.

You should also keep items that don't use electricity at all such as pens and paper, candles, kerosene lanterns and whistles. These things will be valuable in a non-electrical world.

You have to remember that self-defense and home defense is very important in a post EMP world. People will be desperate and things will probably get ugly and some point. So make sure that you have the means to defend yourself and anyone you may be looking after. I would highly recommend some kind of gun. If you're in an area where you can't keep a gun then air rifles and gas powered pistols are widely legal without a license.

Other self-defense items such as sprays, batons and monkey fists are also viable options that will increase your chance of defending yourself successfully. Again, I go into this in more detail in my Bugging In and Home Defense book.

So my advice for long term EMP survival is to print out or get hard copies of any information you think you will need. Also stockpile food and medical provisions and have a bike for each member of your family in case you need to bug out for any reason. Also, get some self-defense items and some other items that don't rely on electricity.

There is one other thing you may want to keep a supply of and that is fuel for your car and your generator if you have one, which leads me nicely onto the next chapter.

11. GENERATING YOUR OWN ELECTRICITY

If you want a way of making your own power after an EMP attack then you will probably want to invest in a generator to supply your household with emergency electricity should you need it.

Of course there is only any need to generate your electricity if electrical items were still working and it was only the electrical grid that went down. So a generator may not even do you any favors anyway unless you have used a Faraday cage to protect the items you will be powering.

When choosing a generator for this purpose, there are a few special requirements you should keep in mind. Firstly you should pick one that runs at a low RPM. This will mean that it will consume fuel at a lower rate than higher RPM generators and also they generally run quieter. This sound level of the generator is important because if people know you have a generator, which also means you have fuel and other people who are desperate will want to take both of these things from you if they know you have them.

Something that you have to remember with a generator is to never run it inside your house. It may be tempting to do this because then other people are far less likely to hear it, especially in the quiet world that would ensue after an EMP attack, but don't do it. Most generators emit dangerous levels of Carbon Monoxide which will build up in an enclosed space and will kill anyone in that area.

A great way to silently generate electricity silently is via solar panels. You can actually get small personal sized solar panels that you can clip into your shoulder strap of a bag for example and it will actually charge your electrical equipment while you're on the move.

Solar panels are actually far more inexpensive these days than you may think. You can get fantastic, very inexpensive items like the Anker Dual-Port Solar Charger that actually folds away to about the size of an ipad for easy storage and transportation. So it's nice and easy to keep in a bug out bag for example.

It is thought that solar panels will survive an EMP because they don't have much circuitry involved. If you go for one of the smaller types however, I would definitely wrap and nest it just to be on the safe side.

12. FINAL THOUGHTS

Well I think that about overs it for this installment!

If you want to stay up to date with my regular free book promotions and to also find out about my future releases you can sign up to my mailing list at - www.southshorepublications.com/steverayder

If you would also consider taking the time to leave me an honest review on this book on Amazon I would be extremely appreciative of your feedback.

You can find links to all of my previous books at - http://www.amazon.com/Steve-Rayder/e/B00U0U3Z3E/ or by searching for "Steve Rayder" on Amazon.

Thanks for reading and I hopefully speak to you all in the next book!